EGG DECORATING!

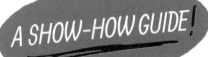

A SHOW-HOW GUIDE!

Written by
Renée Kurilla
&
illustrated by
Keith Zoo

ODD DOT • NEW YORK

Hey there!

This **Show-How** gives you the know-how on egg decorating. We've included only the essentials so you can easily master the FUN-damentals. With a little practice, you'll soon be designing some dazzling eggs! Ready? Let's go!

Don't eat the eggs from chapters 2 and 3!

TABLE OF CONTENTS

NOTE:
To start, you'll need 1 dozen eggs—or more! Both brown and white eggs work great, but white eggs will create more saturated colors. Before you begin, follow the steps on the next page to hard-boil your eggs. The rest of the materials vary for each activity. Check the list at the start of each project.

GETTING STARTED:
HOW TO HARD-BOIL EGGS

Ask an adult to help you with this!

MATERIALS NEEDED:

LARGE POT

OVEN MITT

SLOTTED SPOON

1 DOZEN EGGS
(KEEP THE CARTON!)

PAPER TOWELS
OR KITCHEN TOWEL

BOWL OF
ICE WATER

1 Place eggs in a single layer in the bottom of a large pot.

2 Fill the pot with cold water until the water covers the eggs by about 1 inch (2.5 cm).

3 Heat the pot on high.

4 When the water reaches a rolling boil, lower the heat to medium and simmer for 12–15 minutes.

TIP: A rolling boil is when a liquid starts bubbling rapidly.

5 Use a slotted spoon to carefully transfer the eggs into a bowl of ice water and cool for 10–15 minutes.

6 Dry the eggs with a clean towel, then gently place each back in the carton.

TIP! It's a good idea to let refrigerated hard-boiled eggs come to room temperature before decorating them. If you don't, a layer of condensation may form on the shell and paint won't adhere as well!

1

FOOD
COLORING
& NATURAL DYES

There are two ways to dye eggs: with food coloring or with natural ingredients. They both have really fun results, though using natural ingredients takes a bit longer!

FOOD COLORING

YOU NEED:

1-Cup (250 ml)
Containers for Each Color

1 Dozen Hard-Boiled
White Eggs

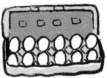

Spoon or Egg Dipper

Teaspoon

Food Coloring

White Vinegar

TIP! If you can find only red, yellow, and blue food coloring, you can use the combinations below to make more colors!

BLUE + YELLOW = GREEN
RED + YELLOW = ORANGE
RED + BLUE = PURPLE

1 Fill a 1-cup (250 ml) container with enough water to cover an egg.

2 Add as many drops of food coloring as you like (10–15 work best).

TIP: The more drops you use, the more vibrant the color will be!

3 Add a teaspoon of white vinegar.

4

STIR!

Repeat steps 1–4 to make as many colors as you like!

5 Gently place an egg on a spoon or egg dipper and carefully lower the egg into the container.

6 Let sit for about 10 minutes.

10:00

TIP: The longer you let the egg soak, the more saturated the color will be!

7

Lift the egg out of the dye and place it back in the carton to dry.

8 Repeat steps 5–7 to make as many eggs as you like!

TIP: Try rubbing a drop of cooking oil on your colored egg with a paper towel. The oil will give your egg a shine!

NATURAL DYES

YOU NEED:

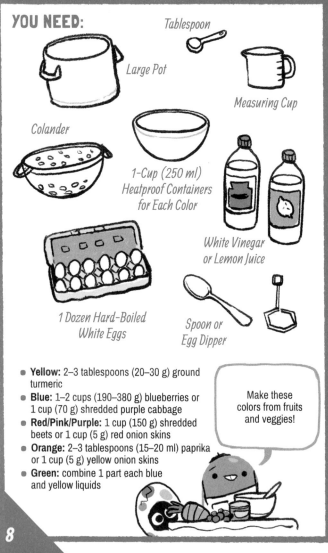

Large Pot

Tablespoon

Measuring Cup

Colander

1-Cup (250 ml) Heatproof Containers for Each Color

White Vinegar or Lemon Juice

1 Dozen Hard-Boiled White Eggs

Spoon or Egg Dipper

- **Yellow:** 2–3 tablespoons (20–30 g) ground turmeric
- **Blue:** 1–2 cups (190–380 g) blueberries or 1 cup (70 g) shredded purple cabbage
- **Red/Pink/Purple:** 1 cup (150 g) shredded beets or 1 cup (5 g) red onion skins
- **Orange:** 2–3 tablespoons (15–20 ml) paprika or 1 cup (5 g) yellow onion skins
- **Green:** combine 1 part each blue and yellow liquids

> Make these colors from fruits and veggies!

1

Pour 2 cups (500 ml) of water into a large pot.

2

Choose which color to make and add the ingredient (for example: red = 1 cup (150 g) shredded beets).

3

Heat the pot on high to bring to a boil.

4

5:00

Boil for 5 minutes, then let the dye cool completely.

5

Strain the dye water through a colander into a container.

6

Add 1 tablespoon (15 ml) of white vinegar or lemon juice.

7

STIR!

8

Repeat steps 1–7 to make as many colors as you like!

9

Gently place an egg on
a spoon or egg dipper.

Carefully lower egg into
the container.

10

Let sit for about 15 minutes.

15:00

11

Lift the egg out of the dye and
place it back in the carton to dry.

12

Repeat steps 9–11 to make
as many eggs as you like!

TIP: After the egg dries,
re-dip it in the same color to
make it more vibrant!

NOW GET CREATIVE! Experiment with some of these extras before you dye your eggs. They make some pretty neat effects!

RUBBER BANDS

1 Wrap rubber bands around your egg.

2 Lower egg into dye container.

3 When the egg is dry, take off the rubber bands!

TAPE

1 Put tape around your egg.

2 Lower egg into dye container.

3 When the egg is dry, take off the tape!

CRAYON

1 Draw a design on your egg with crayon.

2 Lower egg into dye container.

3 The wax repels the dye!

WHIPPED CREAM

1

Spread whipped cream on a baking sheet, then add drops of different-colored food coloring throughout.

2

Use a toothpick to swirl the colors—but don't swirl too much!

3

Roll your eggs in the colored cream until they are completely covered, then let them sit.

4

20:00

After 20 minutes, rinse off your eggs.

5

Let them dry in the carton. They'll have a cool tie-dye effect!

TIP: You can also practice different dipping techniques, like these:

- Dip only the bottom of an egg in one colored dye, then flip and dip the top in another color for a two-tone egg. Try to touch only the non-dyed part of the egg when you flip. If your fingers get dirty, wipe them on a paper towel.
- To create especially unique hues, re-dip your dyed, dry egg in a different color!

2

PAINT

 You can use paint to decorate your eggs! However, if you do, please use your eggs for decoration only. No eating!

YOU NEED:

1 Dozen Hard-
Boiled Eggs
(dyed or not)

Newspaper or
Old Tablecloth

4 or 5 Colors of Acrylic
or Craft Paint

Paintbrush

Toothbrush

1–3 Kitchen
Sponges

Palette or
Paper Plate

Collection of
Leaves

Aluminum Foil
(7"x7"/18 x 18 cm sheet)

Bubble Wrapping
(5"x5"/13 x 13 cm sheet)

Nontoxic Markers

PAINTBALL EGGS

1 Lay newspaper over your workspace.

2 Choose 4 or 5 colors of acrylic or craft paint and squeeze a little blob of each onto your palette.

3 Pick one as your base color and paint your egg, then let dry for a few minutes.

4 Use a sponge to blot a new color onto your egg.

5 Let dry for a few minutes, then use a new sponge to repeat with a different color.

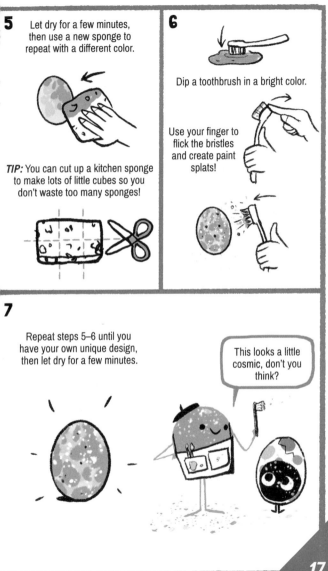

TIP: You can cut up a kitchen sponge to make lots of little cubes so you don't waste too many sponges!

6 Dip a toothbrush in a bright color.

Use your finger to flick the bristles and create paint splats!

7 Repeat steps 5–6 until you have your own unique design, then let dry for a few minutes.

This looks a little cosmic, don't you think?

STAMPED EGGS

1

Lay newspaper over your workspace.

2

Choose your favorite color of acrylic or craft paint and squeeze a little blob onto your palette.

3

Take a leaf from your collection and lay it flat on the newspaper.

18

4

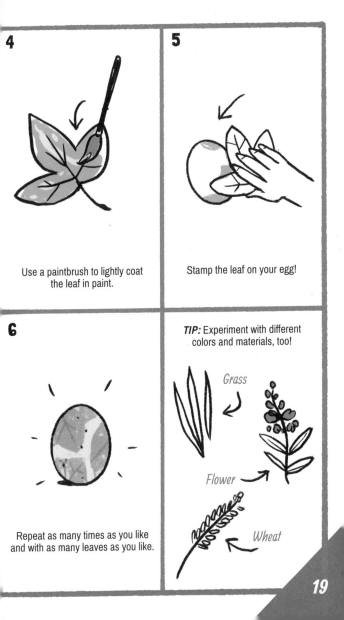

Use a paintbrush to lightly coat the leaf in paint.

5

Stamp the leaf on your egg!

6

Repeat as many times as you like and with as many leaves as you like.

TIP: Experiment with different colors and materials, too!

Grass

Flower

Wheat

EGG WRAPS

1 Lay newspaper over your workspace and a sheet of bubble wrapping or aluminum foil on the newspaper.

2 Choose 2 or 3 colors of acrylic or craft paint and squeeze a little blob of each onto your palette.

3 Use a paintbrush to dab a few colors of paint all over the bubble wrapping or aluminum foil.

4

Lay the egg in the middle.

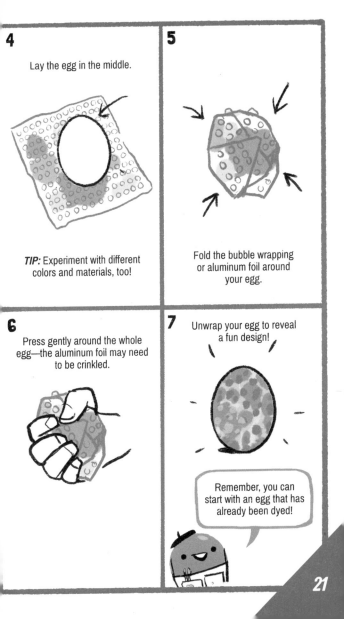

TIP: Experiment with different colors and materials, too!

5

Fold the bubble wrapping or aluminum foil around your egg.

6

Press gently around the whole egg—the aluminum foil may need to be crinkled.

7

Unwrap your egg to reveal a fun design!

Remember, you can start with an egg that has already been dyed!

EGG PEOPLE

1

Lay newspaper over your workspace.

2

Choose 2 or 3 colors of acrylic or craft paint and squeeze a little blob of each onto your palette.

3

Hold your egg in your hand so the larger side is on top. Brush one color around the top half. Let it dry for a few minutes and FLIP! These are your egg person's clothes.

TIP: You can also use an egg that was dyed with the dip method instead of painting this step!

4 Choose a new color and, using a clean paintbrush or nontoxic marker, paint one of these shapes on the top of your egg.

5 Now it's time to draw a face in the middle.

6 Finish off your egg by adding clothing details.

You can make a whole egg family!

3

GLITTER, GLUE & GLITZ

 Make your eggs sparkle, but if possible, try to be eco-friendly! You can find biodegradable or even edible materials! (Just don't eat these eggs if you use anything that's not edible.)

YOU NEED:

1 Dozen Hard-Boiled Eggs
(dyed or not—or if you'd prefer to keep
your eggs forever, try wooden eggs!)

Craft, Edible, and
Glow-in-the-Dark
Glue

Paintbrush

Newspaper or
Old Tablecloth

Palette or
Paper Plate

Glitter

Tissue Paper
(solid colors or patterns)

Scissors

Small Felt
Pom-Poms

Sequins

Wax Paper

2 or 3 Colors of
Embroidery Floss

SPARKLY EGGS

1

Lay newspaper over your workspace.

2

Use a paintbrush to spread glue over your entire egg.

3

SHAKE! SHAKE!

Sprinkle glitter on your egg before the glue dries.

4

20:00

Set the egg down on a sheet of wax paper and let dry for about 20 minutes.

There are *lots* of ways to make your eggs stand out. Try these ideas, too!

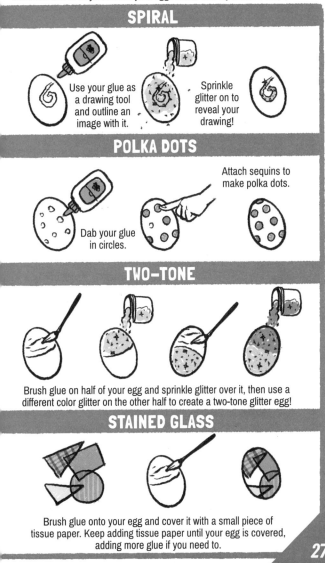

SPIRAL

Use your glue as a drawing tool and outline an image with it.

Sprinkle glitter on to reveal your drawing!

POLKA DOTS

Attach sequins to make polka dots.

Dab your glue in circles.

TWO-TONE

Brush glue on half of your egg and sprinkle glitter over it, then use a different color glitter on the other half to create a two-tone glitter egg!

STAINED GLASS

Brush glue onto your egg and cover it with a small piece of tissue paper. Keep adding tissue paper until your egg is covered, adding more glue if you need to.

27

GLOWY EGGS

1

Lay newspaper over your workspace.

2

Squeeze a little blob of glow-in-the-dark glue onto your palette.

TIP: You might also find glow-in-the-dark glitter glue!

3

Use a paintbrush to spread glue over your entire egg.

4

Set it down on a sheet of wax paper to dry for about 20 minutes.

20:00

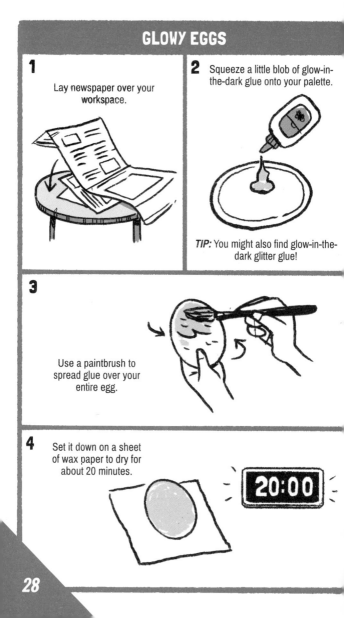

5

When your egg is dry, hold it up to a light for 30 seconds.

:30

6

Turn out all the lights and watch it GLOW!

FUZZY EGGS

1 Lay newspaper over your workspace.

2 Dab a spot of glue on your egg.

3 Gently place a felt pom-pom on the glue.

4 Repeat steps 2–3 until your egg is covered in fuzzy pom-poms!

Get creative with these. Maybe the pom-poms are the hair for your egg person!

EGG SWEATER

1

Lay newspaper over your workspace.

2

Choose 2 or 3 colors of embroidery floss.

3

Use a paintbrush to spread glue on your entire egg.

4

Starting at one end, wrap one color of embroidery floss around your egg 10–15 times.

5

Cut the string and press the end into the glue to secure.

6

Switch colors and repeat steps 4–5 until you cover your egg.

TIP: Experiment with different widths and colors!

31

4
CUT-PAPER CRAFTS

Let's make some
EGGimals and v**EGG**ies!

YOU NEED:

1 Dozen Hard-Boiled Eggs
(dyed or not)

Paper
(white, pink, orange, yellow, black & green)

Scissors

Ruler

3 Paper Towel or Toilet Paper Tubes, Cut to 1½" (4 cm)

Blue, Green & Yellow Nontoxic Paint

Paintbrush

Craft Glue

Nontoxic Markers
(black, pink & green)

2 Black Pipe Cleaners, Each 1½" (4 cm) Long

8 Medium-Size Googly Eyes

BUNNY EGG

1 Cut 2 outer ears from white paper:

2" (5 cm)

½" (1 cm)

2 Cut 2 inner ears from pink paper:

1½" (4 cm)

¼" (.5 cm)

3 Cut a nose from pink paper:

½" (1 cm)

4 Cut a zigzag line at one end of a toilet paper tube. This is your grass!

→

5 Paint your grass green and set it aside to dry.

6 Place a white egg inside the grass tube.

↓

→

7

Apply glue to assemble
the ears like this:

8

When the ears dry, fold the bottoms.

9

Apply glue, and place
ears on top of your egg.

Hold them in place
for a few seconds.

10

Apply glue to the
back of the nose
and place in the
middle of your
egg. Hold the
nose in place for
a few seconds.

11

Using a marker,
draw eyes and whiskers
on your bunny.

TIP: You can apply glue
to the backs of googly
eyes and place those on
your egg instead!

BUMBLEBEE EGG

1
Paint or dye an egg yellow and let it dry.

2
Cut stripes out of black paper.

5 ½"
(14 cm)

¼"
(.5 cm)

3
Cut wings out of white paper.

2"
(5 cm)

½"
(1 cm)

4
Cut a zigzag line at one end of a toilet paper tube. This is your grass!

5
Paint your grass green and set it aside to dry.

6 Apply glue to assemble the stripes around your egg like this:

×2

7

Set your egg sideways inside the grass tube.

8

×2

Loop the pipe cleaners around your finger to curl.

9

●×2

Apply glue to the bottoms of the 2 pipe cleaners and place a googly eye on top of each. These are your antennae!

10

×2

Let the glue dry, then apply more glue to the back of each googly eye antenna and press it onto your egg.

11

×2

Fold the bottom of each wing and apply glue to the bottom, then place each wing on the top of the egg.

12

Use a pink marker to draw cheeks and a black marker to draw a smile on your bee!

CHICK EGG

1

Paint or dye an egg yellow and let it dry.

2

Cut a beak out of orange paper.

¼" (.5 cm)
½" (1 cm)

3 Cut 2 feet out of orange paper.

×2

2" (5 cm)
½" (1 cm)

4 Cut a belly out of orange paper.

1½" (4 cm)
1" (2.5 cm)

5 Cut 2 wings out of yellow paper.

×2

2" (5 cm)

6 Paint a toilet paper tube yellow and set it aside to dry.

7

Spread glue on the back of the belly and affix it to the toilet paper tube.

8

Fold the feet, apply glue to the inside fold, and place underneath the tube bottom. Hold in place for a few seconds.

9

Set your egg inside the tube.

10

Apply glue to the back of the beak and place in the middle of your egg. Hold in place for a few seconds.

11

×2

Apply glue to the backs of the wings and place on the sides of your tube.

Hold in place for a few seconds.

12

Use a marker to draw eyes on your chick.

TIP: You can apply glue to the backs of googly eyes and place those on your egg instead!

RADISH EGG

1

Dye half an egg pink and let it dry.

2

Cut a leaf shape out of green paper.

2" (5 cm)

3

Cut a second leaf shape out of green paper.

1½" (4 cm)

4

Use a green marker to add details to your leaves.

5

Fold the bottoms of each leaf.

6

×2

Apply glue to the folded piece and affix to the top of the egg.

7

Apply glue to the back of 2 googly eyes and press onto your egg. Hold in place for a few seconds.

×2

8

Use a black marker to draw a smile on your radish.

Use pink to add cheeks if you want!

9 Experiment with different leaf shapes and egg colors to make more fruits and veggies! Here are some examples:

Lemon
(yellow)

Pineapple
(yellow)

Strawberry
(red)

Carrot
(orange)

Beet
(pink)

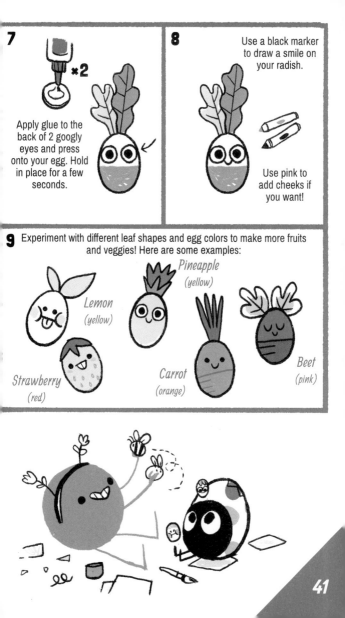

5
WHAT TO DO WITH YOUR EGGS

Now that you have all these COOL eggs, you're probably wondering what to do with them. Here are some ideas to get you started! What ideas do YOU have?

EGG HUNT

Hide eggs all over your living room or yard and invite your friends over for an egg hunt. Give everyone a little basket to collect the eggs they find. Whoever finds the most eggs wins!

For an extra incentive, paint one of the eggs **gold** and give the person who finds that one some extra points!

EGG BASKET

Use decorative grass and display your eggs together in a basket. They always seem to look prettier in bunches!

MAKE A SCENE

Use decorative grass or hay to make a farm scene. You can glue popsicle sticks together to make a fence!

EGG TAPPING

This works best with hard-boiled eggs that have been dyed (not painted, glued, or glittered). First, everyone chooses a favorite egg and a partner. Grip your eggs at the widest point, then start pecking the pointy side of your eggs together!

The last person to have an uncracked egg wins!

If your egg cracks, you're out.

TINY FLOWER POT

Have you ever seen those tiny flower pots at craft stores? What if you put a painted egg in one of those? What kind of characteristics would your egg take on?

EAT THEM!

Here are some tips for making sure your hard-boiled eggs stay edible:

1 Make the eggs a few days in advance and store them in the refrigerator if you can't begin decorating right away.

2 Hard-boiled eggs are typically good for one week in the refrigerator if you plan to consume your creations.

s	m	t	w	th	f	s

3 Eggs that crack during the boiling process can be test eggs to peel and cut to see if the rest are cooked through.

MOM'S STUFFED EGGS

1. *Peel and halve 1 hard-boiled egg.*

2. *Scoop yolk into a small bowl. Add ½ tsp (2.5 ml) mustard (any variety is fine).*

3. *Add ½ tsp (2.5 ml) pickle juice.*

4. *Add 1 tsp (5 ml) mayonnaise.*

5. *Stir until well blended.*

6. *Scoop yolk mixture back into egg white halves.*

7. *Sprinkle the tops with paprika and a pinch of salt.*

YUM!

An imprint of Macmillan Publishing Group, LLC
120 Broadway, New York, NY 10271 • OddDot.com

Library of Congress Cataloging-in-Publication Data is available.
ISBN 978-1-250-78436-0

Editors: Justin Krasner & Kate Avino
Designer: Christina Quintero

Our books may be purchased in bulk for promotional, educational, or
business use. Please contact your local bookseller or the Macmillan
Corporate and Premium Sales Department at (800) 221-7945 ext. 5442
or by email at MacmillanSpecialMarkets@macmillan.com.

Show-How Guides is a trademark of Odd Dot.
Printed in China by Hung Hing Off-set Printing Co. Ltd., Heshan City,
Guangdong Province
First edition, 2022

10 9 8 7 6 5 4 3 2 1

The publisher and author disclaim
responsibility for any loss, injury,
or damages that may result from
a reader engaging in the activities
described in this book.

Keith Zoo and Renée Kurilla

are a husband-and-wife artist/author team living
in Massachusetts. See more of their work online
at keithzoo.com and kurillastration.com, and on
Instagram and Twitter @keithzoo and
@reneekurilla.